FLYING LIGHT TWINS SAFELY

FOREWORD

The purpose of this series of Federal Aviation Administration (FAA) Aviation Safety Program publications is to provide the aviation community with safety information that is informative, handy, and easy to review. Many of the publications in this series summarize material published in various FAA advisory circulars, handbooks, other publications, and various audiovisual products produced by the FAA and used in its Aviation Safety Program.

Some of the ideas and materials in this series were developed by the aviation industry. FAA acknowledges the support of the aviation industry and its various trade and membership groups in the production of this series.

Comments regarding these publications should be directed to the National Aviation Safety Program Manager, Federal Aviation Administration, Flight Standards Service, General Aviation and Commercial Division, Aviation Safety Program Branch, AFS-803, 800 Independence Avenue, SW, Washington, DC 20591.

FLYING LIGHT TWINS SAFELY
Richard W. Carlson, FAA Central Region

The major difference between flying a light twin and a single engine airplane is knowing how to manage the flight if one engine loses power. Safe flight with one engine inoperative (OEI) requires an understanding of the basic aerodynamics involved as well as proficiency in single engine flight. This booklet deals extensively with the numerous aspects of OEI flight. You are cautioned, however, not to place undue emphasis on mastery of OEI flight as the sole key to flying light twins safely.

THE NORMAL TAKEOFF

For normal takeoff planning, pilots should use the manufacturer's recommended rotation speed (Vr) or lift-off speed (Vlof). If no such speeds are published, a minimum of Vmc plus five knots should be used for Vr. For a rule, light twins should not be airborne before reaching Vmc.

After lift-off, the next consideration is to gain altitude as rapidly as practicable. After leaving the ground, altitude gain is more important than achieving an enroute climb airspeed. The airplane should be allowed to accelerate in a shallow climb to attain Vy, the best both engine rate of climb speed. Vy should be maintained until a safe single engine maneuvering altitude, typically at least 400 feet AGL, has been achieved. (If Vy would result in a pitch attitude in excess of 15 degrees, consider limiting the initial pitch attitude to 15 degrees to minimize control difficulty if an engine is lost.) Then a transition to an enroute climb can be made as climb power is set.

Landing gear retraction should occur after a positive rate of climb is established, but not before reaching a point from which a safe landing can no longer be made on the runway or overrun remaining.

THRUST ASYMMETRY

Loss of power on one engine creates both control and performance problems. The control problems include the need to counteract:

- Yaw. Loss of power on one engine creates yaw due to asymmetrical thrust.
- Roll. Loss of power on one engine eliminates propeller blast over the wing. This affects the lift distribution over the wing causing a roll toward the inoperative engine.

The yaw and roll forces must be counteracted by a combination of rudder and aileron.

Zero Sideslip

Sideslip is the angle with which the relative wind meets the longitudinal axis of the airplane. In all-engine flight with symmetrical power, zero sideslip occurs with the ball of the slip-skid indicator centered. Pilots know this as coordinated flight. In OEI flight, zero sideslip occurs with the ball slightly out of center, towards the operative engine.

In OEI flight, there is no instrument that will directly tell the pilot that the airplane is being flown at zero sideslip. It must be placed in a predetermined attitude of bank and ball deflection. In the absence of a yaw string, the suggested zero sideslip configuration at Vyse for most light twins is approximately two to three degrees of bank toward the operating engine, with the ball displaced about one-half of its diameter from center, also towards the operating engine.

OEI flight with the ball centered and the remaining engine providing any appreciable power is never correct due to the sideslip generated. AFM/POH performance figures for OEI flight were determined at zero sideslip, although that fact may not be expressly stated.

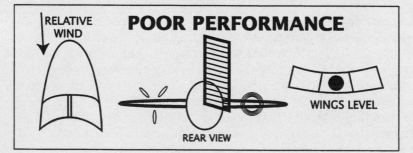

Figure 1. The result of rudder-only correction.

Figure 2. The result of bank-only correction.

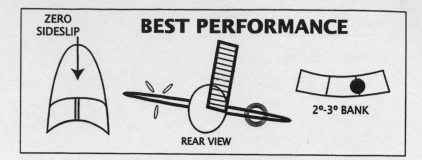

Figure 3. Asymetrical thrust counteracted by both rudder and aileron input.

THE CRITICAL ENGINE

The critical engine is the engine whose failure would most adversely affect the performance or handling qualities of the airplane. On twin engine airplanes with both engines turning in conventional, clockwise rotation (viewed from the cockpit), the left engine is critical. At cruise airspeed, the thrust line of each engine may be considered to be the propeller hub.

At low airspeeds and high angles of attack, the effective thrust centerline shifts to the right on each engine because the descending propeller blades produce more thrust than the ascending blades (P factor). The more power, the greater the effect. The right shifting thrust of the right engine operates at a greater moment arm (distance from the airplane center of gravity) than the left engine. Thus the right engine produces the greatest yawing moment and requires the most rudder to counteract the adverse yaw.

Some twins of more recent design use a counter rotating right engine to eliminate the critical engine. Handling qualities are the same regardless of which engine fails on these airplanes.

KEY AIRSPEEDS FOR SINGLE ENGINE OPERATIONS

Minimum Control Speed (Vmc)

Vmc is designated by a red radial line near the low speed end on most airspeed indicators. Under the small airplane certification regulations currently in effect, the flight test pilot must be able to (1) stop the turn that results when the critical engine is suddenly made inoperative within 20 degrees of the original heading, using maximum rudder deflection and a maximum of five degrees angle of bank into the inoperative engine, and (2) thereafter, maintain

5

straight flight with not more than a five degree angle of bank. Under current 14 CFR part 23 small airplane certification rules, Vmc is determined with:

- Maximum available takeoff power,
- Propeller windmilling in takeoff pitch (or feathered if equipped with autofeather),
- Most unfavorable (aft-most) center of gravity and maximum takeoff weight (or any lesser weight necessary to show Vmc),
- Landing gear retracted,
- Wing and cowl flaps in the takeoff position,
- Trimmed for takeoff,
- Airborne, out of ground effect.

The results are then plotted for a variety of altitudes and extrapolated to a single, sea level value. The twin you are flying may or may not have been certificated under exactly these rules—the airplane flight manual/pilot's operating handbook (AFM/POH) will state the certification basis.

Vmc varies with each of the above factors. The Vmc noted in practice or demonstration, or in actual OEI operation, could be less or even greater than the published value. With other factors constant, Vmc is highly sensitive to bank angle. It is reduced significantly with increases in bank angle and it is increased significantly as the wings approach level. Tests have shown that Vmc may increase more than three knots for each degree of bank less than five degrees. Loss of directional control may be experienced at speeds almost 20 knots above published Vmc when the wings are held level.

The determination of Vmc by flight test pilots in airplane certification is solely concerned with the minimum speed for directional control under one very specific set of circumstances. It has nothing to do with climb performance, nor is it the optimum airplane attitude, bank angle, ball position, or configuration for best climb performance. Many light twins will not maintain level flight near Vmc with one engine inoperative.

Best Single Engine Angle of Climb Airspeed (Vxse)

Vxse is used only to clear obstructions during OEI initial climbout as it gives the greatest altitude gain per unit of horizontal travel. It is invariably a slower speed than Vyse, and may be just a very few knots above Vmc. Even at Vxse the climb gradient will be paltry.

Best Single Engine Rate of Climb Airspeed (Vyse)

Vyse is designated by a blue radial line on most airspeed indicators. It delivers the greatest gain in altitude per unit of time, with the airplane in the following configuration:

- Inoperative engine propeller in the minimum drag position (feathered),
- Maximum power on the remaining engine,
- Landing gear retracted,
- Wing flaps in the most favorable (best lift/drag ratio) position,
- Cowl flaps as required for engine cooling,
- Airplane flown at zero sideslip.

Drag from a windmilling propeller, extended landing gear, flaps extended beyond optimum, or any sideslip will reduce or even eliminate what modest single engine performance may exist. Turbulence and maneuvering of the airplane will further erode performance. When operating above the airplane's single engine ceiling, Vyse will deliver the least possible rate of sink (drift down).

Safe, Intentional One Engine Inoperative Speed (Vsse).

Vsse, often referred to as safe single engine speed, is the minimum speed at which intentional engine failures are to be performed. This speed is selected by the manufacturer to reduce the accident potential from loss of control due to simulated engine failures at inordinately slow airspeeds. No intentional engine failure in flight should ever be performed below Vsse.

SINGLE ENGINE RUNWAY REQUIREMENTS

Consult the performance charts of the AFM/POH. The newer manuals will show:

- Accelerate-Stop Distance. The runway required to accelerate to either Vr or Vlof (as specified by the manufacturer), and assuming an engine failure at that instant, to bring the airplane to a complete stop.

- Accelerate-Go Distance. The runway required to accelerate to either Vr or Vlof (as specified by the manufacturer), and assuming an engine failure at that instant, to continue the takeoff on the remaining engine and climb to a height of 50 feet.

These figures were obtained under ideal flight test circumstances. It is unlikely that they would be duplicated under real-world conditions. There is no guarantee that under all conditions a light twin would be capable of continuing a takeoff and climbing out after an engine failure. You should know, before taking the runway, if the airplane could reasonably be expected to continue its climb following an engine failure.

SINGLE ENGINE CLIMB PERFORMANCE

Climb performance is dependent upon an excess of thrust (power) over what is required for level flight. Loss of power on one engine represents a 50 percent loss of thrust but often an 80 to 90 percent loss of climb performance, sometimes more.

The current 14 CFR part 23 single engine climb performance requirements for reciprocating engine twins are as follows:

- More than 6,000 pounds maximum certificated takeoff weight and/or Vso more than 61 knots: the single engine rate of climb in feet per minute at 5,000 feet MSL must be equal to at least $.027 \, Vso^2$. For twins type-certificated February 4, 1991 or thereafter, the single engine climb requirement is expressed in terms of a climb gradient, 1.5 percent.

- 6,000 pounds or less maximum certificated takeoff weight and Vso 61 knots or less: the single engine rate of climb or climb gradient at 5,000 feet MSL must simply be determined. The rate of climb could be a negative number. There is no requirement for a positive single engine rate of climb at 5,000 feet or any other altitude.

Rate of climb is the altitude gain per unit of time, while climb gradient is the actual measure of altitude gained per 100 feet of horizontal travel, expressed as a percentage. An altitude gain of 1.5 feet per 100 feet of horizontal travel is a climb gradient of 1.5 percent.

With regard to climb performance, the light twin with one engine inoperative will perform marginally at best, and may not be capable

8

of climbing at all under existing conditions. There is no requirement that a light twin in the takeoff or landing configuration be able to maintain altitude, even at sea level, with one engine inoperative.

Airspeed

Best single engine climb rate is found at Vyse with maximum available power and minimum drag. After the flaps and landing gear have been retracted and the propeller of the inoperative engine feathered, a key element in extracting best climb performance lies in minimizing sideslip.

SINGLE ENGINE CEILINGS

The single engine service ceiling is the altitude at which twins can no longer climb at 50 feet per minute in smooth air, with one engine feathered, at maximum certificated takeoff weight. The single engine absolute ceiling is where the rate of climb is zero.

The single engine service ceiling should be reviewed prior to each flight to determine if the airplane, as loaded, can maintain appropriate minimum IFR or VFR altitudes following loss of an engine.

ENGINE FAILURE AFTER LIFTOFF

The manufacturer's recommended procedures for an engine failure shortly after liftoff can be found in the AFM/POH for the specific make and model. However, certain basic procedures follow below. Complete failure of an engine after liftoff can be broadly categorized into one of three scenarios:

Landing Gear Down

If the failure occurs prior to selecting the gear to the up position, it is recommended that the pilot close both throttles and land on the runway or overrun remaining.

Landing Gear Selected Up, Single Engine Climb Performance Inadequate

When operating near or above the single engine ceiling and an engine failure is experienced shortly after liftoff, a landing must be accomplished on essentially whatever lies ahead. The greatest hazard in an OEI takeoff is attempting to fly when it is not within the performance capability of the airplane to do so.

A recent study revealed a very high success rate of off-airport engine-inoperative landings when the airplane was landed under control. The same study also revealed a very high fatality rate in stall-spin accidents when the pilot attempted flight beyond the performance capability of the airplane.

Landing Gear Selected Up, Single Engine Climb Performance Adequate

If the single engine rate of climb performance is sufficient to continue flight, there are four areas of concern to be addressed. In order of precedence, they are:

- Control. Rudder and aileron should be used, aggressively if necessary, to counteract the yaw and rolling tendencies. At least five degrees, and up to ten degrees angle of bank should be used to maintain directional control. The pitch attitude for Vyse should be assumed.
- Configure. The memory items from the "Engine Failure After Takeoff" checklist should be promptly executed to configure the airplane for climb with minimum drag.
- Climb. Maintain Vyse. Reduce the bank angle to that of zero sideslip. In the absence of specific AFM/POH recommendations, a bank of approximately two to three degrees and a ball displacement of about one-half of the ball diameter from center should be made. The bank angle and ball displacement will both be toward the operative engine.
- Checklist. Upon reaching 400 feet AGL, refer to the printed checklist. Review the "Engine Failure After Takeoff" checklist items. If workload permits, then accomplish the "Securing Failed Engine" checklist items to turn off systems and accessories no longer required.

```
┌─────────────────────────────────────────────────┐
│            ENGINE FAILURE AFTER TAKEOFF           │
│                                                   │
│   Airspeed.......................................Maintain Vyse │
│   Mixtures...................................................RICH │
│   Propellers....................................HIGH RPM │
│   Throttles.................................FULL POWER │
│   Flaps..............................................UP │
│   Landing Gear.....................................UP │
│   Identify............................Determine failed engine │
│   Verify.......................Close throttle of failed engine │
│   Propeller—failed engine.....................Feather │
└─────────────────────────────────────────────────┘
```

Figure 4. Memory items from a typical "Engine
Failure After Takeoff" checklist.

ENGINE FAILURE DURING CRUISE

The inflight engine failure generally allows more time for diag-
nosis of the problem with a view towards remedying the situation,
if possible. A logical and orderly check of gauges, switches and systems may rectify the problem without resorting to engine feathering.
As with any single engine operation, declare an emergency with
ATC.

ENGINE INOPERATIVE APPROACH AND LANDING

The OEI approach and landing should be flown as nearly as possible to a normal approach and landing in terms of key positions,
altitudes and airspeeds. The approach and landing may be conduct-
ed with no more than partial flaps, or full flaps may be selected
when on short final with the landing absolutely assured. Large or
sudden applications or reductions in power are to be avoided. The
airplane will float somewhat in the roundout for landing without
the drag of both windmilling propellers, particularly if the flaps
have only been partially extended.

Every effort should be made to execute the approach and landing
successfully the first time. To be avoided above all is a single engine
go-around. From a landing configuration with any degree of extended flaps, the light twin will need an excessive amount of altitude to
transition from a descent to a climb with gear and flaps retracted.

MINIMUM CONTROL AIRSPEED (V_{MC}) DEMONSTRATION

For a Vmc demonstration, an altitude should be selected that will allow completion of the maneuver at least 3,000 feet AGL. The following assumes a conventional light twin with non-counter rotating engines, where the left engine is critical.

With the landing gear retracted and the flaps set to the normal takeoff position, the airplane should be slowed to approximately 10 knots above Vsse or Vyse (whichever is higher) and trimmed for takeoff. An entry heading should be selected and high RPM set on both propeller controls. Power on the left engine should be throttled back to idle, and power on the right engine advanced to the takeoff setting. Pilots must be alert for the stall warning horn, if so equipped, or watch for the stall warning light. The left yawing and rolling moment of the asymmetrical thrust is counteracted primarily with right rudder. A bank angle of five degrees (a right bank angle, in this case) should also be established to assist directional control.

While maintaining entry heading, the pitch attitude is slowly increased to decelerate at a rate of one knot per second (no faster). As the airplane slows and control effectiveness decays, the increasing yawing tendency should be counteracted with additional rudder pressure. Aileron displacement will also increase in order to maintain five degrees of bank. An airspeed is soon reached where full right rudder travel and a five degree bank can no longer counteract the asymmetrical thrust, and the airplane will begin to yaw uncontrollably to the left.

The moment the pilot first recognizes the uncontrollable yaw, or experiences any symptom associated with a stall, recovery should be initiated by simultaneously reducing power sufficiently on the operating engine while decreasing the pitch attitude as necessary to stop the yaw. Recovery is made with a minimum loss of altitude to straight flight on the entry heading at Vsse or Vyse, as symmetrical power is set. The recovery should not be accomplished by increasing power on the windmilling engine alone.

With normally aspirated engines, Vmc decreases with altitude as reduced power available results in less asymmetrical thrust. Stalling speed (Vs), however, remains the same. Except for a few models, published Vmc is almost always higher than Vs. At sea level there is usually a margin of several knots between Vmc and Vs, but the margin decreases with altitude, and at some altitude, Vmc and Vs are the same.

Where Vs is encountered at or before Vmc, the departure from controlled flight may be quite sudden, with strong yawing and rolling (spinning) tendencies toward the idle engine. Therefore, during a Vmc demonstration, if there is any indication of an impending stall such as a stall warning light or horn, airframe or elevator buffet, or rapid decay of control effectiveness, the maneuver should be terminated immediately, the angle of attack reduced as the throttle is retarded, and the airplane returned to entry airspeed. Light twins are not approved for spins and their spin recovery characteristics are generally quite poor.

When stall indications are reached prior to Vmc, the demonstration can still be accomplished by artificially limiting the amount of rudder input to less than full travel. This technique is further described in the FAA's practical test standards.

TRAINING RECOMMENDATIONS

Regular training and practice with a qualified instructor is essential for proficiency in any airplane.

- Thoroughly brief simulated engine failures in advance. The pilot under instruction should know how such failures will be introduced, and what action is expected in response. Unannounced engine failures are suitable only in testing and checking scenarios, and when both pilots have agreed to such before the flight.
- Low altitude engine failure practice is never worth the risks involved. Multiengine instructors should approach simulated engine failures below 400 feet AGL with extreme caution; failures below 200 feet AGL should be reserved for simulators and training devices.
- All simulated engine failures below 3,000 feet AGL should be accomplished by smoothly retarding the throttle.
- Recognize that aircraft systems knowledge is critically important. Practice systems failures too, including partial panel instrument training.
- Occasionally practice OEI flight with a yaw string to observe bank angle and ball position for zero sideslip, particularly at Vyse.
- Do not alter the airplane configuration on the runway after landing unless there is a clear operational need. A striking number of inadvertent landing gear retractions have occurred when the pilot intended to retract the flaps.

SUMMARY

Know the key airspeeds for your airplane and when to fly them. Become thoroughly familiar with the AFM/POH recommended procedures and the checklist, particularly the memory items.

In OEI flight, know the different bank angles for your airplane and when to fly them:

- Five to ten degrees of bank to initially assist the rudder in maintaining directional control in the event of an engine failure, as the pitch attitude for Vyse is established,
- A five-degree bank during the Vmc demonstration required for the practical test for a multiengine class rating,
- Approximately two to three degrees of bank with the ball slightly displaced towards the operative engine to achieve zero sideslip for best climb performance at Vyse.

Know the AFM/POH performance capabilities for your airplane under the proposed flight conditions, and factor in significant margins to adjust for real-world performance. Review:

- accelerate-stop distance,
- accelerate-go distance,
- single engine service ceiling,
- expected OEI rate of climb,
- terrain or obstacles in the flight path.

Know the basic OEI emergency procedures common to all conventional light twins:

- Control. Maintain directional control with rudder and aileron. Assume the pitch attitude for Vyse.
- Configure. Execute the memory items from the "Engine Failure After Takeoff" checklist.
- Climb. Assume the bank angle and ball position for zero sideslip and maintain the best climb rate at Vyse.
- Checklist. Review and accomplish any remaining checklist items appropriate to the situation.

Finally, practice with a qualified flight instructor at regular intervals. The modern, well equipped light twin can be a remarkably capable airplane under many circumstances. But, as with any aircraft, it must be flown prudently by a current and competent pilot to achieve the highest level of safety.

Bibliography

Aarons, Richard N. "Always Leave Yourself An Out," *Business and Commercial Aviation* Vol. 33, No. 1, July 1973

Bervin, Lester H. "Engine-Out Characteristics of Multiengine Aircraft," unpublished staff study, Federal Aviation Administration, December 15, 1980

Byington, Melville R., Jr. "Principles to Bank On," *AOPA Air Safety Foundation Flight Instructors' Safety Report* Vol. 15, No. 2, April 1989

Byington, Melville R., Jr. "Engine-Out Booby Traps for Light Twin Pilots," *AOPA Air Safety Foundation Flight Instructors' Safety Report* Vol. 19, No. 2, April 1993

Kelly, William P., Jr. "Multi-Engine Stalls," *The Aviation Consumer* Vol. XIX, No. 11, June 1, 1989

Kelly, William P., Jr. When Twins Turn Nasty," *Aviation Safety* (three-part series) Vol. XII, No. 19, October 1, 1992, Vol. 20, October 15, 1992 and Vol. 21, November 1, 1992

Newton, Dennis W. "Light-Twin Engine Out Flying," *Business and Commercial Aviation* Vol. 68, No. 11, November 1987

Schiff, Barry J. *The Proficient Pilot* New York: Macmillan, 1985 and *The Proficient Pilot, Volume I* Newcastle, WA, Aviation Supplies & Academics, Inc. 1997.

This is a Back
to Basics,
Aviation Safety
Program Product.

Federal Aviation Administration
Aviation Safety Program (AFS-803)
800 Independence Avenue S.W.
Washington, D.C. 20591

Contact your local FAA Flight Standards District
Office's Safety Program Manager for more safety
information.

U.S. Department of Transportation
Federal Aviation Administration
Washington, D.C.